Printed in Great Britain
by Amazon

61181939R00119